Poems of the
Unrequited

To the
beautiful Amanda,
With much love,

Amy Rainbow

xxx

Poems of the Unrequited

by Amy Rainbow

Illustrations by Kamala Todd

Poems of the Unrequited
Amy Rainbow

Published in 2011 by Aspect Design,
Malvern, Worcestershire, United Kingdom.

Designed and Printed by Aspect Design,
89 Newtown Road, Malvern, Worcs. WR14 1PD,
United Kingdom
Tel: 01684 561567
E-mail: books@aspect-design.net
Website: www.aspect-design.net

ISBN 978-1-905795-86-4

All poems © Amy Rainbow.

(Photo by Shani Stocker.)

Amy Rainbow lives in a sparkly cottage on the western slopes of The Malvern Hills. She is a qualified philosopher, but no longer remembers why.

www.amyrainbow.co.uk

Amy Rainbow – Writer

★ ★ ★ ★ ★

All pictures © Kamala Todd.

Artwork from original paintings.
kamaladuk@btinternet.com
Commissions, portraits and cards.

★ ★ ★ ★ ★

Acknowledgements

With huge thanks to my dad for telling me stories and
writing poems with me when I was a child,

to Lindsay Stanberry-Flynn for making me write again as an adult,

to Marue Fitch, Caitlin Belgard and Neil Collins
for giving me my first opportunities to perform,

to all the cool writers and poets I've met along the way,

to my wonderful family and inspirational friends for
their support, encouragement and general loveliness,

to Kamala Todd for her gorgeous artwork,

and to you.

For my mum.

Although she wouldn't have liked the rude bits.

Contents

Self Mastery

A spate of dates has come of late,
They're coming at a steady rate.
She finds it hard to concentrate
She has so many on her plate.
Attempting to accommodate
Each suitor, every candidate
Takes time, you must appreciate,
And time she simply can't create.
She calculates and allocates
A night for each, and then collates
Her findings and won't hesitate
To strike off any second-rate
Or grating men who irritate
For patience isn't her best trait.
She tends to circumnavigate
The ones who can't communicate
And wouldn't even contemplate
A man who tries to dominate,
Indoctrinate or castigate
A woman. She won't tolerate
A man who likes to agitate
Or one who's constantly irate.
And God forbid she finds a mate
Who's almost past his use-by date.

One day, so she anticipates,
She'll find a man who'll captivate.
Her happy heart will palpitate
And she, in love, will celebrate.
Until that day she'll devastate
And play the game she loves to hate
With men whom she exasperates,
Emasculates, annihilates,
Whose lust at first she cultivates
But then fails to reciprocate.
She does not mean to vacillate,
To lead them on or titillate.
At times she underestimates
Their deep desire to penetrate
Her fortress, and she makes them wait –
Their base desires she will not sate,
Libidos she won't satiate,
Preferring rather to frustrate.
When stars come out and night is late
And stirring hearts accelerate
With one last kiss she seals their fate
And sends them home to master self-control.

John Cooper Clarke

I was dazed and confused when the email came,
They were offering fifteen whole minutes of fame.
I stared at the words, read them twenty times through,
This was crazy, a wind-up, too good to be true.
I rebooted my brain, made myself a sweet tea,
Read the message again, fucking hell, they mean me!
My big break, my main chance, time for making my mark,
They want ME to support bloody John Cooper Clarke!

I downed my sweet tea, then I downed all my gin,
Made a list of the friends that I needed to ring
With my awesome, astounding, astonishing news.
Of the poets on earth, John's the one that I'd choose.
'Bloody hell,' they all said, 'That's amazing, well done.'
They were staggered, impressed, well, except for the one.
'I'm sorry,' she said, 'but I'm still in the dark.
Just remind me again, who's this John Cooper Clarke?'

I maintained my composure although it was hard;
Surely *everyone's* heard of him, Salford's great bard?
I said, 'He's the one with the hair and the face,
He married a monster from outer space,
He's the tall skinny poet with opinions and flair,
Any decent punk gig in the past, he was there.
This is quite a big deal, it's no walk in the park
Getting up on the stage before John Cooper Clarke.'

I said, 'What d'you mean, the name rings a bell?
This man's bigger than Jesus and Lennon as well,
He's been gigging for decades, his poems subvert,
He's spent ten years of life in an open necked shirt.
His stuff is political, scathing and fun,
Satirical, lyrical, brimming with puns,
He likes rhythm and rhyme. What a laugh, what a lark –
Little me, LITTLE ME and John Cooper Clarke!'

Now my moment has come and I'm standing right here
At the pinnacle of my poetic career.
From now on is the only direction downhill?
Bugger that! I'll employ my entire force of will,
I'll go out of my way, yes I'll go to great lengths
To ensure to write more and to play to my strengths.
Watch this space, watch your backs, I'm about to embark
On a highlife of verse thanks to John Cooper Clarke.

★ ★ ★ ★ ★

*that's the best poem
I've ever seen...
...and I've got a
library card!*

Garden Lover

I keep him in the garden shed,
Make sure he's watered, warm and fed,
And in return he tends my lawn –
My Mellors, but without the brawn.
I marvel as he spreads his seed,
Uproots my brambles, scythes my weeds,
And when he wants to prune my rose
I love to help him hold his hose.
I tend the morning glory when
It's getting out of hand again.
And what delight I feel when his
Green fingers stroke my clematis.
We trial each raised bed in turn,
The birds and bees have much to learn
On how to while away the hours
Communing with our passionflowers.
Buds blossom forth, sweet nectar runs,
But will it still when winter comes?
Will he still wish to root and toil,
Dig deep in my infertile soil?
Will burrowing my furrows stop
When earth is cold and leaves have dropped?
Will boggy borders, muddy mire
Extinguish our once flaming fire?
As seasons pass I fear he'll see
That I'm no Lady Chatterley.

My secret garden, moist and warm
Falls derelict, untouched, forlorn.
Forbidden fruit which once so pleased
Lies dry, discarded, dull, diseased,
And leafy glades once lush and cool
Conceal nightshades, reveal the fool.
Wisteria slumps over sheds,
Hysteria at what lies dead.
For when the summer sunshine fades
Our lives will take on darker shades.
This place will bloom no more if he
Should dare neglect *my* shrubbery.
And only I'll know why and how
He's pushing up the daisies now.

Wooed To Wayfaring

Wandering Wayfarer, whence have you sprung?
Your power ascends as you draw down the sun.
Its crimson gold fire drips down through the leaves
As the forest bows down to you, urged by the breeze.

Dancing and laughing you wander the earth,
No sorrow can touch you, your life blessed with mirth,
And new constellations are forged in dark skies
While the moon smiles upon you with lust in her eyes.

Beauty and wisdom unrivalled, untouched
By the passing of time which turns all else to dust.
Eternity's yours and all heaven is too,
Wandering Wayfarer, take me with you.

Infected

It's a danger of the dating game,
A hazard of our age.
I imagine it was common
When free love was all the rage.
I'm contagious, I'm infected,
But I shouldn't be ashamed.
I took every due precaution
So you see I can't be blamed.
The nurse said it spreads easily
And I said it's the pits
When you take a brand new lover
And your lover gives you nits.

It's a proper infestation,
The itching drives me mad,
And I think I've passed them on
To both my sisters and my dad.
That cream the chemist gave me
Was supposed to kill them dead
But I swear I feel each mouthpiece
As it chomps into my head.
It's me against the head lice –
A battle of our wits;
Life has taken on new meaning
Since my lover gave me nits.

I've tried lavender conditioners
And poisonous shampoos,
An electrocuting comb
Which cost a bomb but was no use.
Now I fear the worst has happened:
One whole week of nasty bites
Means the creatures in my hair
May have a claim to squatters' rights.
The scratching stops me sleeping
And my life's falling to bits.
Yes, my sanity's in peril
Since my lover gave me nits.

I *may* have lost the battle
But I won't give up the war.
I have scissors and a razor
And I know just what they're for.
Is it my imagination
Or do head lice squeal in shock
As I hack another handful,
As I shave another lock?
Now I've made up with my lover,
And I guess you'd call us quits –
I gave him a big verruca
Because he gave me his nits.

Sand

Written on Porthcurno Beach.

There's sand in my sandwich and hurt in my heart,
It's now forty eight hours that we've been apart
And I'm sure that you're right and all couples need space
But I miss you like mad all alone in this place.

There's sand in my sandwich, distress in my soul,
Eight days seem an age without you here to hold.
The meals are amazing and as for the pool…
But I won't swim alone, dear – I'd feel such a fool.

There's sand in my sandwich, a spring in my step,
I've resolved that this holiday's not over yet.
I'll explore the whole island with us two in mind,
Then next year we can *share* all the gems that I find.

There's sand in my sandwich, unease deep inside,
Yes, of course I forgive you but, darling, you lied.
I checked on the net to see just what I'd missed
But your fishmongers' conference doesn't exist.

There's sand in my sandwich, a chill in my bones,
You were vague and evasive today when I phoned.
If it's really a matter of cash you should say
As you know without question I'd happily pay.

There's sand in my sandwich, dark thoughts in my dreams,
But I'm blowing this out of proportion, it seems.
Even Mum said today you're a sensitive bloke
And it's sweet that you're spending each night at my folks'.

There's sand in my sandwich, no solace in sleep
So I lie in the dark and in silence I weep
At the things that you said when I asked if it's true
That you miss me in *quite* the same way I miss you.

There's sand in my sandwich, revenge on my mind.
You're a cad, she's a slapper – you're two of a kind.
This jug of sangria's gone straight to my head
And I told that young waiter I wished you both dead.

There's sand in my sandwich but joy in my heart.
You were right: a clean break, pastures new, a fresh start.
So you're shagging my sister – big deal, your loss;
Now I've hooked up with José I don't give a toss.

Playing With Fire

A Cautionary Tale Relating To The Hazardous Pursuit Of Juggling

I have a friend whose eldest son
Took up a hobby, just for fun;
He started juggling with three balls
But found no challenge there at all.
To him it came so easily,
Such soothing rhythms - one, two, three -
That soon he yearned for something more,
So learned a pattern using four.
Yet still feeling dissatisfied
His thoughts, they turned to trying five.

Not wishing for his balls to drop
The practice sessions did not stop.
He promptly mastered five, then six -
Amazed his friends with fancy tricks,
And, this success gone to his head,
He chose to juggle rings instead.
His chums were stunned by all the things
He did with spangled, spinning rings.
Despite their eager yells and whoops
He shortly tired of hurling hoops.
So naturally he next progressed
To juggling clubs, and was impressed
At his unrivalled grace and skill -
The tossing gave him quite a thrill.

Proficient in the basics now,
He sought out moves he thought would wow
His pals, not knowing they would kill
To have a fraction of his skill.
All green with envy, how they'd like
To be as talented as Mike.
(For Michael was this young man's name -
His dad and grandad called the same.)
Under the leg, behind the back -
However hard, he'd get the knack.

But soon he felt like aiming higher
And took to juggling clubs of fire.
Then, for the ultimate in kicks,
He lit not four, not five, but six,
And hurled them high into the air
So passers-by would stop and stare,
Entranced at such a sight to see,
Enthralled by his dexterity.

Adept at throwing on the spot,
Young Mike began to wonder what
Fresh challenges there were to set
When inspiration struck: he'd get
A unicycle - it would feel
Fantastic cycling on one wheel!
And then, his sense of balance sound,
He juggled as he rode around.

Now, once maneuvering expertly
He thought how awesome it would be
To put a show on in the town
And have the public gather round.
They'd praise his polished, deft routine,
He'd be the best they'd ever seen!

That Friday evening, after dark,
He set out for the busy park.
(There'd been some musical event,
With bands and food and beer tent.)
The sight of all those people scared
Poor Mike - no longer sure he dared
Perform his act to all these folk -
What if they saw him as a joke?
And so, afraid his nerve would fail,
He quickly quaffed five pints of ale.
Then, keen to swiftly make a start
Before his courage could depart,
His paraffin-soaked clubs he lit
Whilst on his cycle he did sit.

As flaming torches lit the skies
The mob let out great gasps and cries.
He wasn't feeling quite his best,
But clearly they were all impressed.
This eager throng, they spurred him on,
They clapped and cheered him, whereupon
A tipsy Michael tried a trick,
Fell off his cycle, then was sick.

The horde shrieked shrilly in lament
As burning clubs fell on the tent.
The canvas caught alight with ease,
And fierce flames, urged by the breeze,
Leapt boldly to the old bandstand
Which, in its heyday, had been grand.
As fire raged up aged oaks
The jam-packed park went up in smoke.
Stunned crowds had to evacuate;
The fire brigade arrived too late.

When sifting wreckage all they found
Was Michael lying on the ground,
And fire-fighters heard him say,
Before he sadly passed away,
'Excuse me, tell me, do you know
If everyone enjoyed the show?'

Now, one thing is quite clear to me -
I'm sure that you won't disagree -
If you should take up juggling
Remember gravity will win.

The moral of this tale is clear:
Don't juggle fire whilst drinking beer.

I Don't – A Polite Refusal

So you want my hand in marriage,
Want my heart till death do part
And you're pushing for an answer
But I don't know where to start.
I feel sick each time I see you,
Overjoyed each time you leave,
You are ugly from the inside out,
Your morals make me heave.
If you held me down at gunpoint
I wouldn't say I do,
If you set yourself on fire
I wouldn't piss on you.
If you have one single good point
It's impossible to spot,
If you needed rope to hang yourself
I'd help you tie the knot,
If you asked me for directions
I'd tell you where to go,
If you ever threatened suicide
I'd come and watch the show.
If you claimed cold words could kill you
I'd calmly call your bluff,
A record-breaking barge pole
Would not be long enough.
If no other man existed
I'd still find a better mate,
If you told me you were dying
I'd help you set the date.

You're less welcome than a dog poo
Trodden on with both bare feet,
More persistent than a pack
Of wild wolverines on heat,
You're the scab I can't stop picking,
You're the boil that just won't burst,
You will *never* be the best man
But you'll always be the worst.
If I threw the biggest party
You'd be bottom on my list,
I despise you, you disgust me,
I presume you get the gist.
If my subtlety confounds you
And my meaning isn't clear
Then you're denser than I realised,
More demented than I feared.
No, I *will* not ever marry you,
I *will* not be your wife,
I would rather swallow glass
And gouge my eyes out with a knife.
You're as thick-skinned as a rhino,
As thick as two short planks,
I'd rather eat my entrails.
In other words – no thanks.

Best Served Hot

They say the way to a man's heart is through his stomach.
Surely a steak-knife through the ribcage
Is quicker and slicker,
More efficient?

Proficient in cooking
But not in love, it seems.
Two streams
Of salty glazing
Ooze from onioned eyes.

The lies!
Twenty years of wedded hell.
Bedded his belle – found a better dish.
I'll make him wish he'd stayed, hadn't strayed.

Our last supper, our last farewell.
A simple pie, a simple man.
I never put much in, but nor did he.

Rabbit – slaughtered – blind eyes staring,
Daring me to see.
So recently bleeding and twitching,
Guts wrenched out, heart stamped upon,
A life sacrificed for a man.

Twenty years brewing and stewing.
Seasoned to flavour.
Savour this hour.
Feel my power.
My first stand, my one and only upper hand.

Said he felt alive again.
So that was death?
No wonder he was so cold!

'Thanks for all those years. Please, no tears.
A second chance to dance the dance.'

Thought he'd drawn his last breath?
Not yet. Wait.
That comes later.

How to pledge eternity and stick it out?
Kick him out? No!
All types of rat named on the box, except mine.

We vowed until death and I took that as truth.
Here's the proof of *my* love.
Still here to serve, give him all he deserves.
He'll see that love hurts, get his just desserts.

And so, soon, my sweet, you'll swoon towards sleep.
Then, gripping and slipping, gliding in, sliding in,
Whose turn *now* for sticking the knife in?

I say *one* way to a man's heart is through his stomach,
But there are more.
I'll take *both* routes
Just to be sure.

Looking At You

You are beautiful
And you make me happy.
I am lost now you are found.
You are the echo to my sound,
You are the sun and I the moon,
You are the axis around which I spin,
You are my everything.

I have places to show you,
Secrets to share.
Can we dare to wish
That this, this bliss, will last forever?
I will never let you down,
I could never be untrue
For you, you are my king and I your queen,
You are the stars, the space between,
You are the taste for which I thirst,
You are my universe.

I gaze at you – my dream come true –
And I am blessed,
For yes, you *are* perfection,
All I need to feed my soul,
An angel sent to nourish me.
You are infinity.

You stand beside me
And I am shaking
For I am making
Attempts to put this into words,
I *must* be heard,
My life, my love,
You *need* to know
And yet,
'Hello,' I begin,
'I don't think we've met.'

★ ★ ★ ★ ★

Shelf

I'm hoping I'm eloping on the twenty ninth of June,
But the man that I'm in love with thinks that June is far too soon.
Well, in fact he told me yesterday he's started having doubts -
He's not sure if we should marry, but I think we'll sort it out.
He just needs some soft persuasion that a wedding would be right,
Though he's acting rather strangely since our row the other night.
He thinks that I'm possessive and obsessive and I'm not;
I just want him to myself for all eternity. And what
On earth is wrong with that, I ask you, when two people are in love
And their union is smiled on by sweet angels up above?
He seemed to be suggesting that he wanted someone else
And that I was just some nutter who was best left on the shelf!
So I rattle round my empty home and watch my silent phone
And I wonder what he's doing while I'm left here on my own.

Come Friendly Bugs

With thanks and apologies to John Betjeman.

Come friendly bugs and fall on Facebook
Wipe out Twitter, kill Myspace. Look
How this evil interface took
Over minds.

Come bugs and blow to smithereens
The drivel showing on our screens
And we'll develop new routines
Which aren't online.

With virtual social networks dead
We'll have to do real life instead,
Leave futile comments left unsaid,
Unread, unseen.

We'll *meet* our friends, go out for drinks
With scant regard for hyperlinks,
We'll *tell* each other what we think
And how we've been.

No typists' thumb to take its toll
Yet rosy cheeked from alcohol
We'll laugh out loud and not type LOL
At random quotes.

No more the dread of friend requests
From colleagues, in-laws, sexual pests,
No shoving our own interests
Down people's throats.

Emoticons will cease to be
And parties will be worry free,
No photos up for all to see
Online next day.

No pokes which your top friend ignores,
No tossers sticking in their oars,
With browsing hours spent out of doors
More time to play.

Although we know it's somehow wrong
We tweet and update all day long,
Post drunken drivel, crappy songs
And stir up strife.

Come friendly bugs and fall on Facebook
Wipe out Twitter, kill Myspace. Look
How this evil interface took
Over life.

Imperfection

I have the perfect boyfriend, he's right in every way,
If we go out to a restaurant he *never* lets me pay.
He's patient and considerate, he's clever and he's kind,
He's all a girl could dream of, he's really quite a find.
He's witty and he's charming, he's handsome, fit and strong,
He *never* contradicts me – not even when I'm wrong.
We have a lot in common, share interests and friends,
And when we are together the laughter never ends.
He's honest and he's faithful, I know he'd never stray,
He's compassionate and caring and I love him more each day.
He listens when I'm talking and really understands.
He shops and cooks and cleans and he likes hugs and holding hands.
He's pretty good at dusting and washes up quite well,
I've never heard him snoring and his armpits do not smell.
He's not a fan of football but likes books and films instead.
He doesn't lose his temper and he never farts in bed.
There's just one imperfection, but I don't mind at all,
It's barely worth me mentioning, it really is so small.
Look, *nobody* is perfect – you have to understand,
So as far as I'm concerned I'd say I've met my ideal man.
He truly is a marvel, apart from that one flaw,
Last week he mentioned marriage – what girl could ask for more?
You want to know the problem? I'm not sure I should say.
If I can overlook it then it might just go away.
What is this imperfection? Ok, if you insist.
His only imperfection is that he does not exist.

Weird Beard

Do you really find it weird
That I bear a bushy beard?
Have you honestly not heard
Of a buxom bearded bird?
If you like your girls hirsute
With a furry back to boot,
Who can save leftover nosh
In their handlebar moustache,
Who with great panache and flair
Plait their ear and nasal hair
And who groom their fluffy feet
Thrice a day to keep them neat,
Then perhaps I am the one -
Let's go out and have some fun.
Take your hat off, let me peek.
Oh my God! You're bald! You freak!

Women's Institute

I am *not* pushing forty, I'm just thirty nine,
Nowhere *near* middle aged, I have plenty of time,
And I swear on my life, yes, I tell you no lie,
You will not catch *me* joining the WI.

I have hobbies and friends, a good job and a car,
I've a husband I love, things are fine as they are.
No, you can not persuade me, so don't even try,
I shall never enrol in the WI.

It's all jam and Jerusalem, knitting and cakes,
My Aunt Vi is so proud of the doilies she makes,
But I'd pull my own teeth out and pigs may well fly
Before I'd set one foot in the WI.

Yes, the magazine's great and the website's not bad
But the members are ancient and lonely and sad.
It's for widows and spinsters, not women like I,
I would not be seen dead at the WI.

Look, it's just a one-off so don't spread it about,
I'd be mortified if my dark secret got out,
But to stop all the nagging and humour Aunt Vi
I shall go along *once* to the WI.

Oh, all right, I admit it, that really was fun,
I can barely believe that this moment has come,
But I have to confess, and please don't ask me why,
I'm considering joining the WI.

We meet once a month in the village school hall
And it isn't all sewing and pickling at all,
You can do what you like and the limit's the sky
Once you've paid up your subs to the WI.

Last week was burlesque and Italian meals
So we baked our ciabattas in basques and high heels,
And the girls in my branch make me laugh till I cry,
I'm completely at home in the WI.

We go rowing and bowling and hiking up hills,
We do yoga for calmness and caving for thrills,
And you must see the crust on my blackberry pie
Now I'm fully ensconced in the WI.

What bizarre preconceptions some people still hold,
They're convinced we're all senile, pathetic and old.
Who succumbs to such prejudiced thinking? Not I!
I'm a member for life of the WI.

There is honestly something for everyone here.
You have nothing to lose; there is nothing to fear.
So come on all you ladies, no need to be shy,
Roll on up, come on down to the WI.

Word Perfect

I'd like to teach the world to rhyme,
Keep poetry alive,
I want this place to be a space
Where spoken word can thrive.
I like my verse accessible,
I want it to be fun,
It shouldn't be elitist,
This stuff's for everyone.
From toddlers to pensioners,
From commoners to kings,
Let's write of love and lunacy
And everyday things.
So what if grammar bores you?
So what if you can't spell?
I've got so much I want to say,
I bet you have as well.
Don't worry if it's nonsense,
Who cares what it's about?
Just open up your mind's trap-door
And see what falls out –
A lullaby, a limerick,
A sonnet or a song,
A rap about a shopping list,
There *is* no right or wrong.
As silly as Spike Milligan,
As chatty as Pam Ayres,
As long as you remember –
Do it *your* way, not theirs.

More misery than Plath could spout,
More cool than Zephaniah,
Get *your* ideas on page or stage
And set the world on fire.
These words, they're not just *my* words,
Would you like them? Shall we share?
Let subconscious thought take over,
Leave our conscious minds elsewhere?
Shall we see where talking takes us
When our brains are disengaged?
We'll make poetry in motion –
Nothing structured, nothing staged.
Let's be seers, let's be prophets,
Fine philosophers and fools,
Let's have anarchy in thinking –
Who needs order? Who needs rules?
We'll use free association,
We'll make poetry a game,
See where rhyme and rhythm take us,
No embarrassment, no shame.
Let us board the bird of lexicon,
May language let us fly.
What I'm saying is, they're OUR words,
We are poets, you and I.

Bird

Inspired by a young Wren's yearning for flight.

I spy a seagull soaring in a sky of azure blue,
Looking down on me with beady eyes just like you used to do.
A peacock fans his feathers, urging everyone to stare,
A reflection of your preening as you'd groom your thinning hair.
Flamingos flurry past me with a high and haughty stance,
Stark reminders of the dread you could instil with just one glance.
Proud pigeons in the park peck half-chewed chips between each strut,
Bulbous bellies reminiscent of your great gargantuan gut.
A squawking cockatiel creates unceasing searing noise,
Unremitting in its echo of the grating of your voice.

Those last words on your deathbed – 'I shall come back as a bird,' –
At the time they sounded ludicrous, conceited and absurd.
But your prophecy proved provident, I fear it has come true,
For each feathered foe encountered has the countenance of you.
They say that those in mourning lose all purpose in their life;
People worry that I'll flounder as your widow, not your wife.
Yet I know your spirit's near me in the body of a fowl
So my life is blessed with meaning by each eagle, every owl,
For with you around in bird-form, my work has just begun:
I shall take aim with my slingshot and I'll slaughter each last one.

Dangerous Verse

The dangers of writing poetry, I find,
Are of losing oneself up one's own behind
And of bruising oneself – all those pats on the back
As one masters the craft and as one gets the knack
Of the metre and form, of the rhythm and rhyme,
Of the beats to a foot and the feet to a line,
Until haiku and rondeau come naturally
And acrostics and sonnets spring effortlessly
From one's brain, through one's hand, via keyboard or pen,
To the feather-white paper; it's finished! And then
It's an audience one needs, to applaud and confirm
That one's worthy of praise for the skills one has learned.
And so when I've perfected my fine masterpiece
I'll perform for my children. Their wonder won't cease
At the talented wordsmith their mum has become
And her dazzling display of great intellect. 'Come,'
I call softly, 'and listen to what I have here.
It's a poem for you two, my offspring most dear.'
So I read my *hilarious* story in verse
About goblins who've cast an unbreakable curse
On a dragon who lives in a mystical cave,
But who's now forced to serve as their miserable slave.
When the dragon has flown and the goblins are slain
I just *know* that my boys will demand it again.
I can see in their faces my tale's gone down well –
It's a mum's intuition, you see, I can tell
That they're proud of their poetess mother, her art,
And I feel great joy and such love in my heart
At the awe in their eyes as they stare up at me,
Until sweetly they chorus, 'Mum, what's on TV?'

★ ★ ★ ★ ★

Oats

I met him when I was working
In a greasy spoon café,
He said it was fate that he'd met me,
That things often turn out that way,
That just when you've given up looking
You could meet the girl of your dreams,
And the woman you've searched half your life for
Is right on your doorstep, it seems.

He was funny and drop-dead gorgeous,
Called me flower and angel and pet,
He asked for my mobile number
But Siobhan said to play hard to get.
And Joanna said don't trust a trucker,
They've a woman in every town,
Take your time, take it slow, get to know him
To make sure that he won't let you down.

He came in twice a week for his porridge
And he did have the gift of the gab,
But he swore he was ready to settle,
Was too old now to play Jack the Lad.
His sweet-talking and charm won me over
And I said I'd go out on a date,
But there'd been some delay at the depot
So he got to the pub an hour late.

We got on like a house on fire
And when it was time to go home
He insisted on coming to my place,
Didn't want me to walk on my own.

So of course he came in for a coffee
And he ended up staying all night
Then he asked me for porridge for breakfast
'Cause he knew that I'd make it just right.

He told me that I was his soul-mate,
That the bond that we had was unique,
That he wanted to make a commitment,
Could he move all his stuff in next week?
And oh, how I loved all the cuddles,
How I swooned at his dreamy blue eyes.
He assured me he'd always be faithful
And he promised he'd tell me no lies.

I liked having someone to care for
And I did all I could so he'd stay,
Did the washing and cooking and cleaning
And I gave him his oats every day.
He told me that I was his princess
So I treated him just like a king
But he gave me no silver to speak of,
He was saving it all for my ring.

When they offered him long-distance haulage
He called it a stroke of luck
But I started to miss all the cuddles
As he'd sleep overnight in his truck.
It's not easy to hold things together
When your partner's away half the time
But he swore if he could he'd be with me
And he vowed that his heart was all mine.

Siobhan said that I deserved better
With my looks and my brains and soft heart,
That he treated me worse than a doormat,
Disrespected me right from the start.
He'd have cut down his shifts if I'd told him,
But it wasn't my place to ask,
So I'd lovingly cook him his porridge,
Send him off with his oats in a flask.

Then this woman rang early one morning,
Said she had something urgent to say,
She told me that she was expecting,
That my Jack had been playing away.
I felt sick with the humiliation,
Oh the shame of it, oh the despair,
Through the whole of our eighteen month courtship
He'd been getting his oats elsewhere.

Siobhan said she'd seen it all coming
And so did my boss and my folks.
They said it was weird and unhealthy
The obsession he had with his oats.
That's the last time I fall for a player,
My heart's battered and tattered and torn,
I shall give up on men altogether
And I'm going to marry Siobhan.

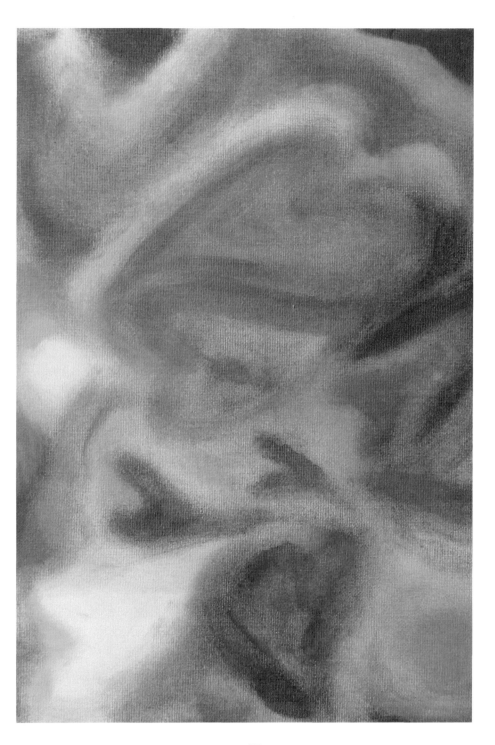

Voyager's Advice

Tu vas en France to find yourself, et oui, pour explorer,
Parisian deals, Elysian fields – les beaux Champs Élysées.
But will your stay be hellish or a perfect paradise?
To help ensure the latter I've a few words of advice...

The French are proud of everything and praise is often sung
Of their culture and their couture, their splendid mother tongue,
Their range of tasty cheeses, from Camembert to Brie,
And politeness is expected, so be sure to say merci.

Vin rouge is cheap and cheerful and pastis has quite a kick
But be careful not to mix them as that may well make you sick.
They don't use francs and centimes, it's euros now and cents,
Yet smiles are welcome anywhere so make sure they're well spent.

To say they smell of garlic and that Frenchmen all eat frogs,
Is as trite as saying Dutchmen live in windmills and wear clogs.
The food will be fantastic almost everywhere you go,
But please avoid the horsemeat and forgo les escargots.

May your travels be tremendous, bringing you beaucoup de joie,
May the stars shine on Les Pyrénées especially pour toi.
So au revoir, mon cher ami, good luck et bon voyage,
Have fun, my merry prankster, young troubadour at large.

Tu vas en France to find yourself, et oui, pour explorer,
But ere you go there's quelque chose that I would like to say:
I hope you have a great time, but please, mon ami fou,
Ne m'oublie pas, while you're away, and I'll remember you.

The Man Who Wore Tweed

I was done running round after pretty young things,
Had enough thrills and spills and the heartache it brings
And although debauched living was plenty of fun
It was high time my life as a nun was begun,
So I dumped all the hair dye, and ditched all the glitz,
Swapped breath-taking corsets for clothing which fits,
Then I popped to the bookshop for something to read
And that's when I met him – The Man Who Wore Tweed.

He was after a book called 'The Mind of Macbeth',
While I wanted romance not madness and death,
But then, as we queued, he defended his choice
With such fire in his eyes, such delight in his voice,
That I wanted to talk and to listen to more
For here was a passionate man, I was sure.
Then for once in my life I let him take the lead
And was asked out for drinks by The Man Who Wore Tweed.

He was old – almost eighteen months older than me –
But had manners and grace, and was gentlemanly.
We chatted for hours, got drunk on champagne
Till the manager threw us out into the rain,
And we laughed and began to walk home through the park
Where we sang in the moonlight and danced in the dark,
And then, when he kissed me, I melted, weak-kneed,
That's the moment I fell for The Man Who Wore Tweed.

He inhabits my dreams and he lights up my days,
He pokes fun at my sesquipedalian ways
And I, in return, make the odd playful swipe
At his trilby and cords, at his slippers and pipe,
But despite seeming utterly, wholly mismatched
We're both ready to end all that 'no strings attached'.
So yes, I confess, I will have to concede
That I'm smitten, bewitched by The Man Who Wears Tweed.

For a change I am sure that my judgement's not wrong,
More distinguished than handsome, more clever than strong,
Quite unlike all the men that I usually meet,
He's a vet who breeds beagles and deals in antiques.
It's a meeting of minds, not libidos and lips,
And I find that his company always outstrips
That of youths living loosely and spreading their seed,
Yes, I'd far rather be with The Man Who Wears Tweed.

He is honest and tactile, he's funny yet deep.
He plays jazz on piano and sings me to sleep.
He's the rarest of finds – a reliable man,
And my friends think it's strange but I don't give a damn
Because what they don't realise and what they can't see
Is he makes me feel safe and he lets me be me.
Now my life is complete; I have all that I need
In my country retreat with The Man Who Wears Tweed.